With The Beatles
The historic photographs of Dezo Hoffmann

EDITED AND DESIGNED BY PEARCE MARCHBANK

THE CAPTIONS IN THIS BOOK ARE TAKEN FROM
AN INTERVIEW WITH DEZO HOFFMANN, JULY 1982.

EDITORIAL ASSISTANT: SALLY PAYNE.
PICTURE RESEARCH ASSISTANTS: HEATHER PAGE, SUE TRITTON.
LAYOUT: ALISON FENTON, MIKE BELL.
ARTWORK: HAZEL BENNINGTON, HILARY SABINE, PHIL LEVENE.
PHOTO PRINTING: REX FEATURES, DEZO HOFFMANN.
TYPESETTING: LAURA BECK TYPOGRAPHY, FOCUS PHOTOSETTING.
PRINT PRODUCTION: ROBERT SAMPSON.
PRINTED IN JAPAN BY DAI NIPPON PRINTING COMPANY, TOKYO.

ISBN 0.7119.0111.2
UK ORDER No. OP 41961

EXCLUSIVE DISTRIBUTORS:
BOOK SALES LIMITED,
78 NEWMAN STREET, LONDON W1P 3LA, ENGLAND.
THE PUTNAM PUBLISHING GROUP,
200 MADISON AVENUE, NEW YORK, NY 10016, USA.
OMNIBUS PRESS,
GPO BOX 3304, SYDNEY, NSW 2001, AUSTRALIA.
MUSIC SALES GMBH,
KOLNER STRASSE 199, D-5000 COLOGNE, WEST GERMANY.

TO THE MUSIC TRADE ONLY:
MUSIC SALES LIMITED,
78 NEWMAN STREET, LONDON W1P 3LA, ENGLAND.
MUSIC SALES CORPORATION,
799 BROADWAY, NEW YORK, NY 10003, USA.

Omnibus Press
LONDON/NEW YORK/COLOGNE/SYDNEY

THE FIRST MANIFESTATION OF BEATLEMANIA. OUTSIDE THE LIVERPOOL EMPIRE, MARCH 24, 1963.

In 1962 Dezo Hoffmann went to Liverpool and took his first pictures of a "smart but rather subdued" group o four young men. He had received a letter from a fan sent to *Record Mirror*, of which Dezo was staf photographer, bitterly complaining that the press was ignoring a "fab" group in Liverpool called The Beatle He spent three days with them and this session resulted in Dezo Hoffmann catching their unique style an energy on film for the first time, and resulted in a friendship that lasted throughout the years of Beatlemania This book shows a selection from the pictures taken by Dezo, both in public and in private, with The Beatle

He took more shots of the group, and was closer to them, than any other photographer. He covered ever major event in their career, often being the only photographer present ... their audition at Abbey Road with George Martin, their first tours of Europe and America, making their first albums, radio shows and films.

Dezo Hoffmann began work in his home country Czechoslovakia as clapper boy in the A-B Studios i

Prague, making *Eroticon* starring Hedi Lamarr. After national service in the army he joined Twentieth Century Fox in Paris and was sent to cover Mussolini's invasion of Abyssinia. Next came the Olympiad Popular in Barcelona, held by the nations boycotting Hitler's 1936 Olympics. Here he witnessed the outbreak of the Spanish Civil War. Joining the International Brigade Press Corps, he was the first newsreel man to send out footage, working alongside men such as Robert Capa and Ernest Hemingway. He was seriously wounded while filming, but followed the retreat to France. With the Second World War mobilisation he joined the Czech army, eventually arriving in England in 1940. He covered nearly all theatres of war as a news cameraman. All his war work has now been donated to the Imperial War Museum, London.

With the end of the War he joined the Crown Film Unit for a while but, as he says, "there was no excitement any more, so I deserted film-making and started in Fleet Street as a freelance photographer, being my own

boss as I was used to.'' He began to specialize in show-biz celebrities ... Charlie Chaplin, Marilyn Monroe,
Louis Armstrong, Frank Sinatra, Marlene Dietrich. In 1955 he joined the weekly music paper *Record Mirror*.
He applied the techniques learnt on the battle field to photographing shows and concerts, TV spectaculars and
pantomime. He almost always used available light, and small format cameras. His rivals were still working
with flashbulbs and cumbersome old plate cameras. He was also amongst the first to use colour film for live
show-biz photography. Dezo Hoffmann is very much the Cartier Bresson of the entertainment world. He
shuns publicity but at the same time gets very close to the thousands of stars he has photographed, creating
everything from the most formal portrait to the most spontaneous behind-the-scenes composition.

In his thirty years of work he has built up a library of over a million negatives. A source of many extensive
pictorial biographies. Many of these pictures have become archetypal images, many more have never ever

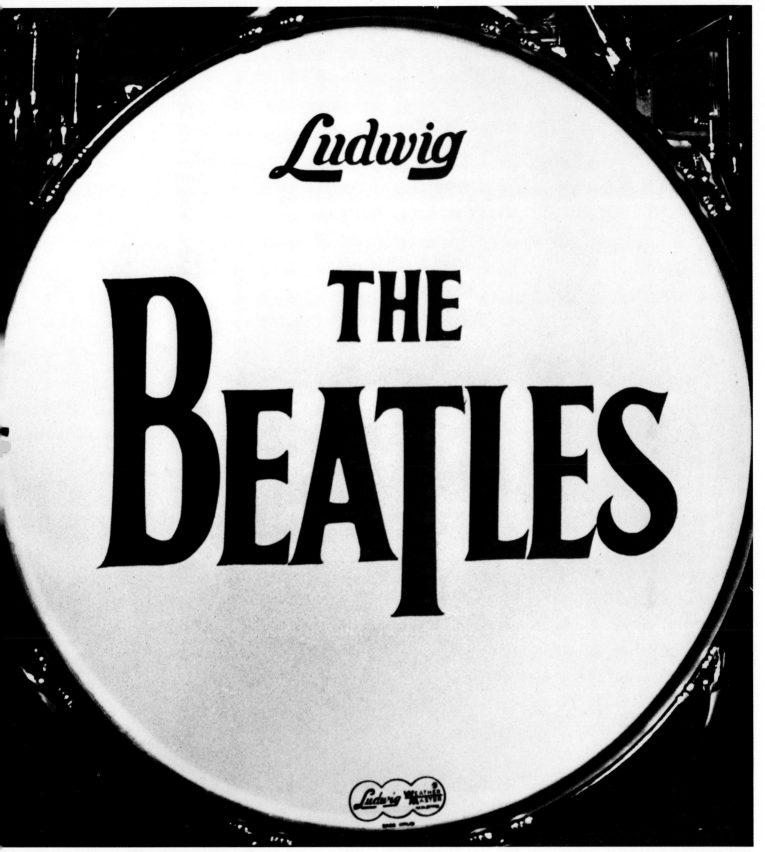

been printed, let alone published. This applies to his vast collection of Beatle pictures. This book can only scratch the surface of what must be one of the most unique photo archives in pop music history, containing as it does many frames taken by the group themselves, even an 8mm colour movie, which must be the first ever film taken of them, also featuring many scenes actually shot by The Beatles.

The Beatles looked up to Dezo in the group's formative years. They were new to the business, but he was on speaking terms with so many of the stars they admired. They respected his advice and it was he, as much as anyone, who helped evolve their unique image. He knew the first day he met them that they had something vital and he wanted to show it to the world ... "to me, a London photographer who knew all the best-known groups very well, I was struck by their sincerity and simplicity". This, Dezo Hoffmann captured in images which have become part of the visual language of the twentieth century. PEARCE MARCHBANK.

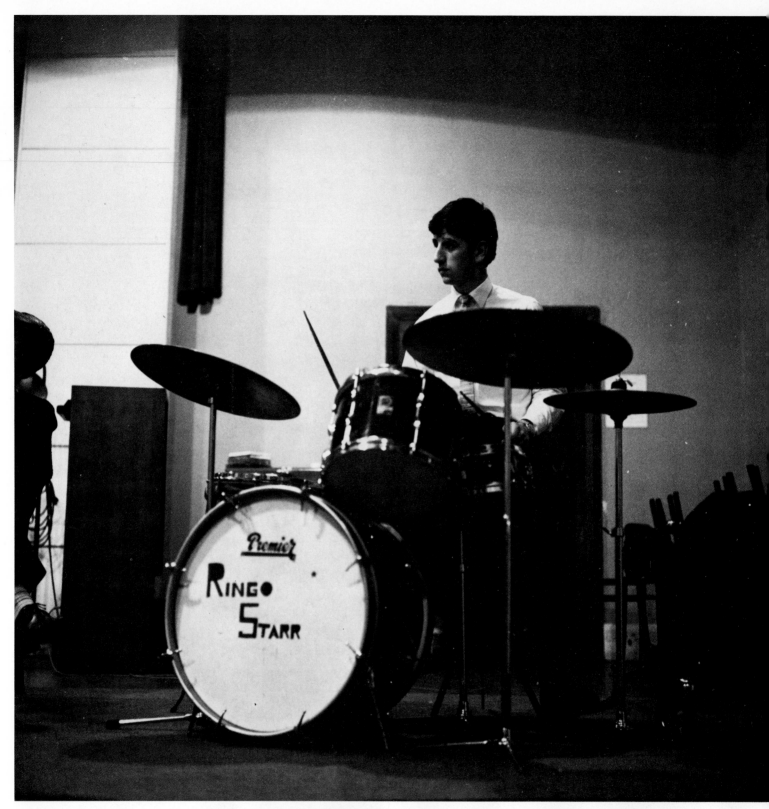

FIRST RECORDING SESSION,
SEPTEMBER 4, 1962, AT ABBEY
ROAD:
*This is the first time they
worked with George Martin.
They were spellbound by his
musicianship. Before, they just
sounded like The Shadows or
anybody.'*

*'Ringo's own drum kit from his
previous group was brought
down from Liverpool. It had
been George Martin's suggestion
to get a new drummer.'*

'Ringo has only been in the group for 18 days, and these were the first professional press pictures to be released. I put all those instruments in the foreground to camouflage George's black eye. There'd been a fight in Liverpool about Pete Best's replacement by Ringo.'

'The old Beatles Vox amplifier
which they bought in Liverpool.
We called their hair really long
then.'

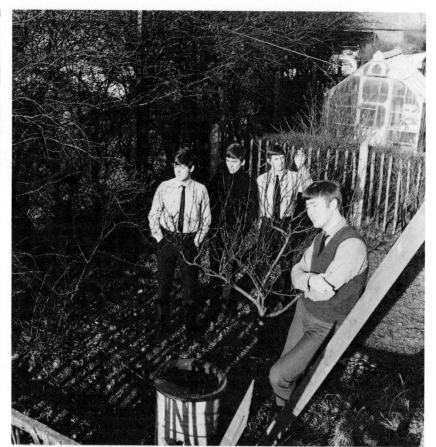

LIVERPOOL APRIL, 1963:
'This was a Record Mirror assignment. A girl had sent a picture to the paper of four young boys with long hair, complaining that we never did features on Liverpool bands. So I went up to Liverpool and they knocked me for seven. They were so fresh, so full of vitality and fun and so honest. When they found out I'd been taking pop pictures since 1953 I became a sort of father confessor to them, and would advise them on how other bands behaved, which they took advantage of. We had a genuine friendship and that's why I stayed with them.'

'This was Paul's father's house. My meeting with them was very special to them and so they dressed smart for me. We planned some little domestic scenes in the house and the garden.'

'After the house session, Paul drove us all out to Sefton Park in Liverpool. He thought he was the King of Siam in that Mark I Cortina. My bag was full of camera equipment and when they saw the cine camera and how easy it was to handle, they started to shoot. This was the first ever film of The Beatles, and shot by The Beatles themselves.'

'This is the famous 'jump' which later became the "Twist And Shout" cover. I wanted to somehow portray the vitality of those boys and I felt these pictures did just that.'

THE CAVERN APRIL, 1963:
'*Taken the same day at the Cavern. Although The Beatles were never to play the Cavern again, I felt some pictures there would be useful. I wanted a working shot to capture the wine cellar atmosphere. The smell of alcohol and sweat was ridiculous down there because there was no ventilation.*'

'*Later Paul and I went to "Mr. Smiths" Nightclub in Manchester. Paul was dying to meet Frankie Howerd so I introduced them, even though Frankie had never heard of The Beatles. The rest of the boys were sorry they hadn't come with us when they heard.*'

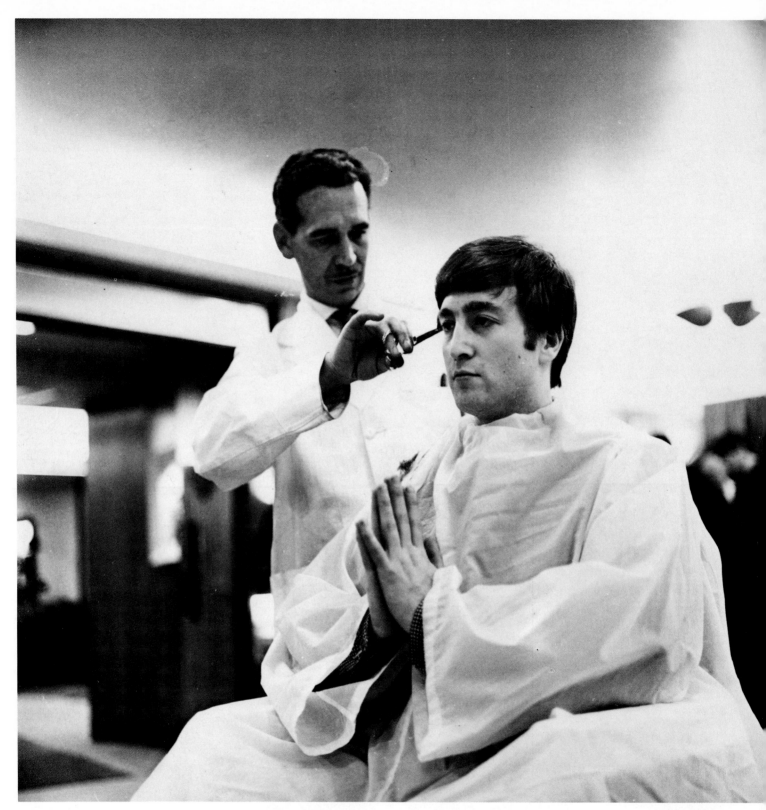

HORNES OUTFITTERS LIVERPOOL
APRIL, 1963:
'The hairdresser was a friend of theirs who liked Astrid Kirchherr's idea of longer hair for The Beatles. He would groom and discipline their hair for them every week.'

'This was a typical Beatles publicity shot. These scenes were my idea because they had no photographic ideas themselves in those days, although they were very photogenic.'

THE EMPIRE LIVERPOOL
24 MARCH, 1963:

'Their first big concert. They were supposed to be supporting Tommy Roe and Chris Montez but by public demand The Beatles were forced to close the show and all the posters in Liverpool had to be changed at the last moment. It was the first time Beatlemania really showed itself on their home territory. I was deafened by the sound of screaming, clapping, and shouting. And outside the theatre there were millions of people, stretching right round to the station. It was the first time I'd ever experienced anything like it.'

'One of the dressing rooms was packed with presents like this from their fans.'

EMI Manchester Square, London. A silver disc presentation for album sales of Please Please Me, 22 March, 1963:

CONCERT AT STOWE SCHOOL APRIL 1963:

'They'd never even seen an English public school before, but after the initial disappointment at it being boys only, they were pleasantly surprised. They realised it was a lot of baloney about public schoolboys being snobs, and talked with the Stowe boys as if they'd always mixed with people like that. It was a change for them after playing to decadent youths in Hamburg nightclubs and they loved it.'

'After the concert they had dinner with the headmaster and his children, and signed autographs for the boys. All the boys were beginning to grow their hair Beatle-style by then, although the craze had only been going a few months.'

'There was no screaming and
the audience stayed seated
throughout, which was a shock
to them. But for the first time
they could hear themselves play
and they really let go — they
would have played on for hours,
they were enjoying it so much.'

'These pictures were an idea to portray them as civilised human beings, because there was a terrible anti-Beatle feeling from adults who felt they were a bad influence on their children.'

'At first neither John nor I liked this picture because it was contradictory to his tidy image. But his expression and the lighting were so good that we ended up liking it. It seems to sum up John at that time.'

ABBEY ROAD 11 FEBRUARY, 1963:
'George Martin's main interest
was that live, they should sound
exactly like their records. He
wouldn't leave them alone for a
second, not even in the canteen.
Once he'd heard the rough
version of each song he'd go
away, work on it musically, and
come in the next day knowing
exactly what he wanted. Being
intelligent, The Beatles would
do exactly that. They never
argued musically, but about
disciplining themselves to get to
the studio on time. Sometimes
one song would be recorded 50
times and then George Martin
and Glyn Johns, the engineer,
would cut it together, staying
late into the night.'

'This picture was originally going to be the cover for "Please Please Me" but it didn't work out.'

BBC Light Programme — "Sounds 63" broadcast live from the Albert Hall April, 1963:
'The only time The Beatles played the Albert Hall, on a bill of stars including Del Shannon, Susan Maughan, Shane Fenton.'

WESTMINSTER CAMERAS, OLD
COMPTON STREET, LONDON.
APRIL, 1963:
'This was the first time they
saw the 8mm movie we'd made
in Liverpool. They were each
given a camera by the shop in
gratitude for their advertising it.
John refused to let me use this
picture because he had his
glasses on and so we did the
whole session again.'

Dezo Hoffmann's studio in
Wardour Street, June 1963:
*'This was a photographic session
showing The Beatles in formal
studio poses. Up to this time all
their photos had been more
candid. I published a book,
"The Beatles" and used some of
these pictures. Soon afterwards,
I was visited by the CID who had
been contacted by the BBC.
Apparently the serial numbers
on the lights corresponded with
those on some they'd had stolen
years before. I'd bought the
studio complete with fixtures
and fittings, and so had to go out
and get a new set of lights.'*

*'At last John let me photograph
him in his glasses. He didn't
want to look posed and was
successful in looking very
natural.'*

'These were all self-portraits in
the dressing room mirror. I tried
to teach them photography
without flash, and these were a
little shaky and out-of-focus.'

'Paul and Jane Asher had only
known each other a few months,
but she helped them a lot to
adjust to London.'

BRIAN EPSTEIN, JULY 1963:
'Brian wanted his own press pictures that he could autograph for the fans. I took them against my better judgement. After all, he was their manager, not one of the group and I reckoned the worst thing he could do was compete with them. But he insisted.'

BBC Maida Vale, recording "Pop Go The Beatles", 18 June, 1963:
'A rare shot of Paul playing around on the drums.'

'The canteen at Maida Vale. I never went for anything arty with them. This is the sort of image I wanted to project, and I slogged at it.'

'It was Paul's 21st birthday and all they could afford for him was the bumps outside the studios in the road.'

CONTACTS (FOLLOWING 8 PAGES)
'I decided that they should and could get established individually, and so did the first split photo session. From then on, we did a lot of single pictures, and other groups started doing it too. A crowd of about 200 girls kept a solid vigil outside all through the session.'

RECORDING "EASYBEAT" AT THE
PLAYHOUSE, 23 JUNE, 1963:
*'This was the first time Ringo
used his famous Ludwig kit in
public. There was only one mike
for the drums.'*

BBC PARIS CINEMA — RECORDING FOR A MIDDAY LIVE RADIO SHOW, JULY, 1963:
'These were gimmicky pictures with Liverpool comedian Ken Dodd for my benefit. They also met Wilfred Brambell there, who was later to appear with The Beatles in "A Hard Day's Night".'

"A Day In The Life", shot in London as a photofeature for the Liverpool Echo, July 1963:

'This was their shirtmaker. I introduced them to him, he was an old Hungarian friend. This was the first time they'd had tailored clothes. They loved it.'

'I took this to capture the sordidness of Soho, because it reminded me very much of Liverpool.'

48

WESTON-SUPER-MARE, 22-27 JULY
1963: THE ENGLISH TOUR WITH
GERRY AND THE PACEMAKERS AND
TOMMY QUICKLY:
*They filmed a lot during this
session and I believe Richard
Lester was inspired by this film
when he directed "A Hard
Day's Night".'

*The Beatles' van that carried
them and all their equipment
from concert to concert.'

'This session was for the American market, which as yet I hadn't been able to penetrate because the Americans didn't want to know about English pop groups. I knew I needed something strong, and since they were on a seaside tour I had the idea of hiring bathing huts, old-fashioned swimming costumes etc. They loved dressing up in silly costumes, John kept his on back at the hotel long after the session was over. The value of those pictures became huge overnight. The Daily Mirror used one as a centre spread, and America went barmy. Everybody in America used those pictures, even though they had barely heard any Beatle records. Over here, Reveille magazine used one of them as a free poster to boost their circulation figures, and it was then I realised I should do a Beatles book, and that I hadn't been wasting my time.'

'We finished the beach session, and it had been so successful that we just wanted to do more. So on the way back we stopped at this go-kart track.'

'These pictures were taken as an advertisement for Ty-Phoo Tea. Each Beatle had to shape a different letter for Ty-Phoo. We had to do it over and over until they got it right.'

FILMING A GRANADA TV SHOW IN
MANCHESTER, NOVEMBER, 1963:
*'Back on their own territory, we
could hardly get the session done
without them being mobbed.
Beatlemania had really started.'*

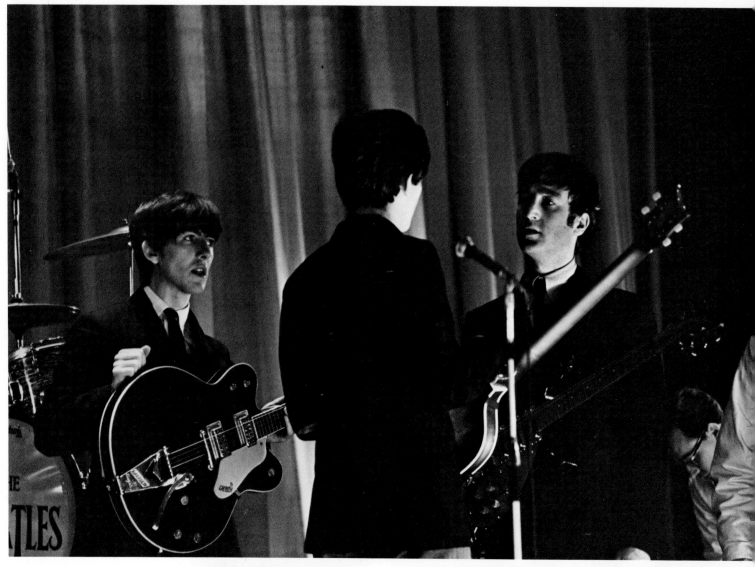

THE ROYAL VARIETY SHOW,
LONDON PALLADIUM,
4 NOVEMBER, 1963:
*'The dress rehearsal for the
concert that was used by the
government to take the spotlight
off Whitehall. The Profumo
affair had just broken in the
press, and the government
squashed publicity by creating
Beatlemania. The press reported
hoards of screaming girls
besieging the Palladium,
whereas in fact there were only
about six girls there.'*

*'There were so many
photographers at the photo call,
which I thought was important
for them, so I made them
recreate the famous jump on the
tiny stage.'*

*'I used to photograph Marlene
Dietrich years before and, to me,
she had then the same innocent
spirit of The Beatles, so I
struggled to get a picture of
them together.'*

ON THE TRAIN TO LIVERPOOL FOR
"JUKE BOX JURY", BBC TV SHOW,
11 DECEMBER, 1963:
*'Neil Aspinall is with them
here, he was their road
manager, and was closer to them
than Epstein. They had a verbal
understanding that the unit
consisted of the four Beatles and
Neil — and nobody could upset
that unit. It was the first time
Juke Box Jury went out from
anywhere but London.'*

"JUKE BOX JURY" FROM THE MOSS
EMPIRE, LIVERPOOL,
11 DECEMBER 1963:
*'They really scored here, and set
the precedent for other bands,
like the Stones, to do "Juke Box
Jury" later. They really were
marvellous entertainers, they
could make fun out of anything
and the kids went stark raving
mad! After the show, they played
a few numbers.'*

At Elstree, recording "The
Morecambe And Wise Show" for
ATV, 2 December, 1963:

'It was easy for them to get
shows like Top Of The Pops,
but they needed to get on the
adult viewing schedules. So the
Morecambe And Wise Show
was perfect. They did just two
numbers.'

'Neil fell asleep in the dressing room and Mal Evans watched critically while they rehearsed.'

'A present from a fan — they kept as much of all that stuff as they could.'

THE BEATLES FAN CLUB CONCERT,
WIMBLEDON PALAIS,
14 DECEMBER 1963:
'A concert strictly for fan club members, and 3000 turned up from all over the country. It was probably the best Beatles concert I ever witnessed and I was frustrated at not being able to capture the atmosphere without a flash. Only two albums had been released then, but the merchandising stall sold out within minutes.'

'Either side of The Beatles, Neil Aspinall and Bryan Sommerville, their Press Officer, kept the crowd in check.'

'They sat behind the bar, which was of course closed, and greeted every single fan individually.'

'It was the first time they used crowd barriers, but Neil ordered them because the boys would have been torn to pieces. The noise was just incredible.'

THE EMI CHRISTMAS PARTY, ABBEY ROAD, DECEMBER, 1963:
'Abbey Road Studio Number One was converted into a reception area and all the EMI artists, entourages, managers, and so on would gather. The Beatles hated these parties but went to meet people they'd wanted to meet for a long time, like Helen Shapiro, Alma Cogan, and other stars of the time.'

'Gerry Marsden, George Martin and George Harrison.'

THE BEATLES CHRISTMAS SHOW,
FINSBURY PARK ASTORIA,
24 DECEMBER, 1963, 11 JANUARY,
1964:
*'Once again they couldn't hear
their music at all for the noise
of the fans. But they enjoyed
dressing up and acting for the
kids.'*

ABBEY ROAD, DECEMBER 1963:
'Paul would often shadow
George Martin to learn about
the technicalities of recording.
Here he sat in on Billy J.
Kramer's studio time as he
recorded the follow-up to "Do
You Wanna Know A Secret".'

BBC Paris Cinema:
'We walked to Cecil Gee's clothes shop in Shaftesbury Avenue from my studio. Whenever we had a bit of time to spare, we'd do some pictures.'

Backstage during Sunday Night At The London Palladium, January, 1964:
'They now had the star dressing room.'

PARIS/ORLY AIRPORT,
14-16 JANUARY, 1964:
*'Ringo missed the plane to
Paris, but arrived the next day.
There were posters all over
Paris displaying the pictures
Astrid Kirchherr had taken in
Hamburg.'*

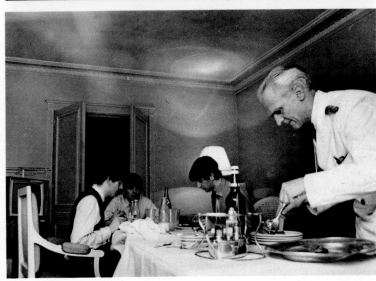

'They tasted crepes suzettes for
the first time and this waiter
did nothing else all day but
make crepes for them.'

'They stayed at the George V
Hotel in Paris and posed
outside, Paul in his Parisian
oilskin coat, with which he
started a whole fashion craze.'

'Paris Match decided they
wanted a big photofeature,
including the cover, to be done
all in one morning. The Beatles
never usually woke up until the
afternoon and I was given the
unfortunate job of waking them
at 9.30am to do the session. I
decided it would be a good idea
for all concerned if we had a
sequence of photos showing them
shaving, dressing etc. I insisted
they cancel a scheduled New
Musical Express interview
because Paris Match was more
important, and since John had
never heard of it he didn't
forgive me for months.'

'They did a walkabout down the
Champs Elysees and it was soon
obvious that they couldn't stop
and have a quiet drink.'

'This was a marvellous day. We were eating in a café with the Parisian Melody Maker correspondent, Mike Hennessey, when I was summoned back to the hotel by Epstein. I took Mike with me and Epstein broke the news that The Beatles had at last cracked the American market — "I Wanna Hold Your Hand" was Number One on the Cashbox chart. This meant it was more than likely they'd be asked to do the Ed Sullivan Show, since they'd been on the shortlist for a while. The stars and stripes portrait was the first picture I took after the news, to commemorate Stateside success.'

'They had an Austin Princess imported from England to travel from the hotel to the Olympia in, for the concert.'

'Backstage and onstage at the Olympia. The Beatles were disappointed with the French in many ways. Firstly because the audience was 95% male, (French parents were strict with their daughters and believed The Beatles to be hooligans). Also, merchandise sales proved that Ringo was by far the most popular Beatle in France. All his pictures would sell out way ahead of the others and his name would be shouted everywhere they went. This caused a little tension within the group because, after all, Ringo was still a session man then. He wasn't yet a fully fledged Beatle.'

'Ringo the ever-aspiring photographer.'

'Ringo with my camera in his dressing room, teaching Olympia co-star Sylvie Vartan, how to take a picture.'

'Impromptu interview — they were almost kidnapped off the street and taken into the studios of Europe 1, France's international radio station. It turned out to be one of their best-ever interviews. The interviewer couldn't speak English. The Beatles couldn't speak French. They just talked.'

LEAVING HEATHROW FOR AMERICA,
7 FEBRUARY, 1964:
*'John and Cynthia had only
recently got married, so she
came too.'*

'Dick James (with the glasses), The Beatles music publisher, bids farewell to his boys, along with lawyer David Jacobs, while Epstein looks on.'

'The pre-flight press conference. Maureen Cleave of the Evening Standard was determined to be photographed with them.'

ARRIVING AT KENNEDY AIRPORT,
THE ED SULLIVAN SHOW, CBS, NEW
YORK, FEBRUARY, 1964:
*'Paul's bemused expression tells
the story. Circling over Kennedy
airport, we could see an
astronomical crowd of people.
There'd never been crowds like
that before — we honestly
thought the President was due to
arrive. In front of Paul is Phil
Spector, who travelled with us
though he did very little with
The Beatles.'*

*'Contrary to popular opinion,
pop stars were given a rigorous
going-over at customs.'*

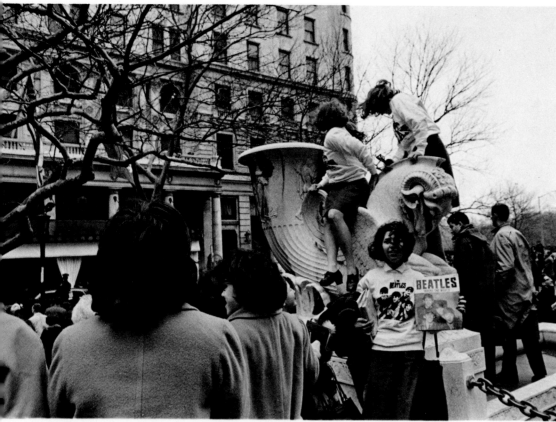

'The crowd outside the Plaza Hotel, New York. The girls were wearing T-shirts (bearing my design) supplied them by Seltaeb, the merchandising company set up for the American tour. Each fan was given a free T-shirt, one dollar and a bus ride to the airport. And that's really how Beatlemania started in America.'

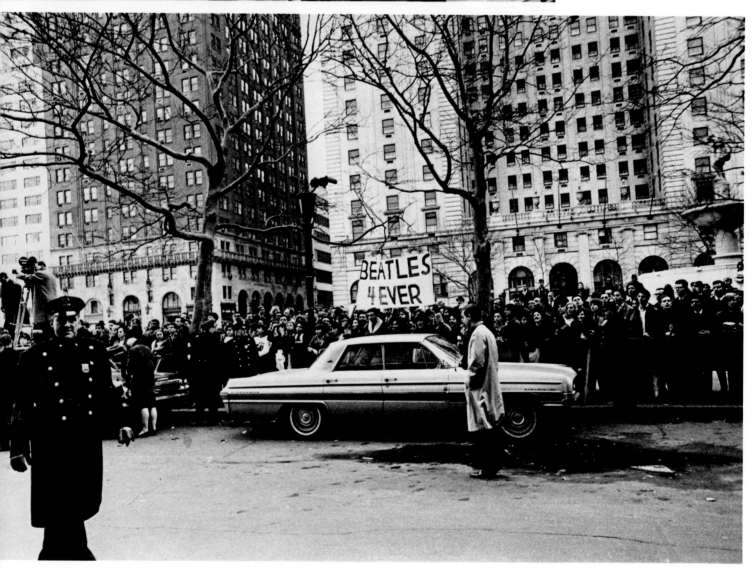

'With Bryan Sommerville in the Plaza Hotel. The Maysle brothers were filming and Ringo looks unusually disconcerted. They had a whole floor reserved at the hotel, including a mail room for the sacks of fan mail that arrived from England every day.'

'The Ed Sullivan show consisted of all British stars that day.'

'The Ed Sullivan show. George was very poorly and stayed at the hotel with his sister looking after him, so they had to use Neil Aspinall for rehearsals.'

*'The local press went crazy on
stage with them and they
insisted Brian Epstein was
photographed with them.'*

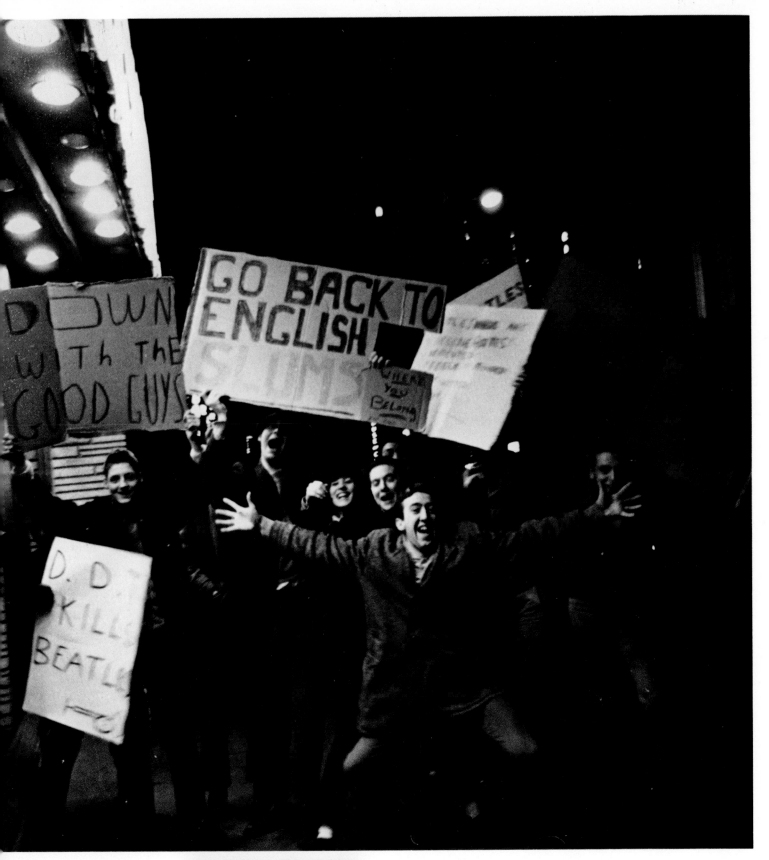

NEW YORK CARNEGIE HALL
CONCERTS 7 FEBRUARY, 1964:
'The queue for the Carnegie
Hall concert was enormous. The
anti-Beatle protesters, who
manifested themselves especially
in Detroit, were there too.'

RESS RECEPTION IN THE NEW YORK
LAZA:
*With Bryan Sommerville
nducting the press conference,
ey weren't at all nervous, even
ough it was coast to coast
ress. Just like they conquered
e, they conquered the whole of
e United States. George
Martin had been worried seeing
e barrage of microphones,
otographers and television
meras. But they used their
yle, sincerity, looks, and won
erybody over.'*

*'On the table is the first US
Gold Disc for "I Want To Hold
Your Hand".'*

'Filming with the Maysles brothers in the Plaza. Brian Epstein allowed them to film on the Washington trip next day, which eventually became a full-length film.'

'They had to have mounted police escorting their car through the crowds. I regret that there were no wide-angle lenses in those days.'

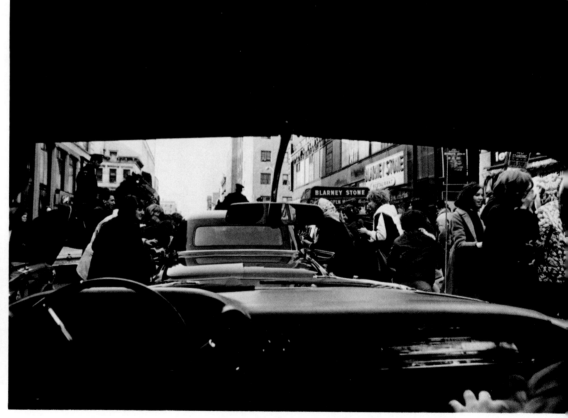

'They managed a walk in Central Park.'

Paul posing for me with George's sister, who lived in America and joined us there.'

'We woke up the morning we were supposed to fly to Washington knee-deep in snow. The Beatles had heard things about American airlines and refused to fly, demanding a train. They coupled a carriage on to the regular Washington train and we got there on time.'

'They were very glad to have gone by train. They saw a little of snow-covered America.'

'I left Ringo with one of my cameras. He was the only good photographer in The Beatles. He also shot with the Maysles' movie camera.'

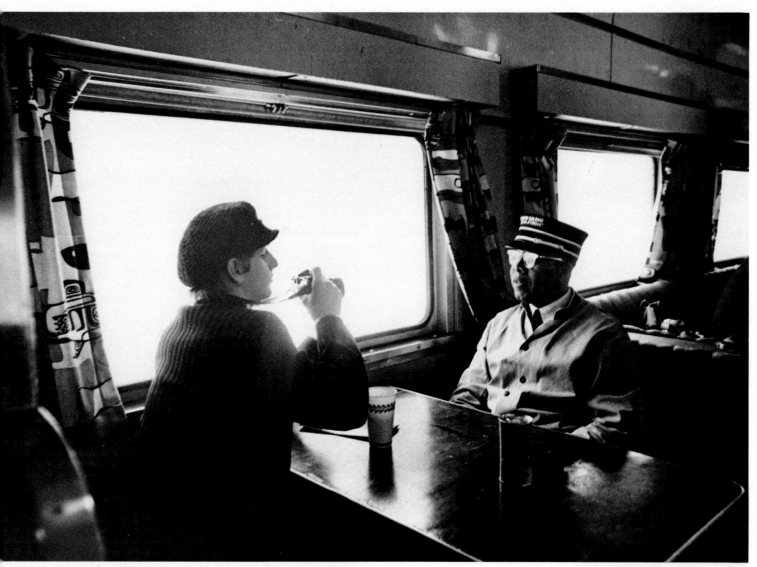

'Ringo made a real friend with
the attendant. George
spontaneously grabbed his hat
and tray. Nothing was ever
posed, it was all ad lib and I
just had to anticipate each time.

'The Beatles are greeted at
Washington station, with a
banner from WWDC,
Washington's local radio
station.'

BEFORE AND DURING THE CONCERT
AT WASHINGTON COLISEUM,
11 FEBRUARY, 1964:
*'They threw millions of jelly
babies on stage after Paul's
comment that he liked them.'*

*'Ringo was on a revolving
platform, so all the audience
had a chance to see him. It took
half an hour for him to recover
from his dizziness.'*

*'They gave a press conference
from the stage before the show
to the international press corps.'*

MIAMI, 13-22 FEBRUARY, 1964:
*'Miami was a remarkable
experience. We had a whole
floor in the Hotel Deauville, and
we also borrowed a villa off a
millionaire. They enjoyed it so
much, you can see in the
pictures there's not one
miserable face. It was as if
they'd been born into it, they
were so nonchalant.'*

'A good review in a local paper.'

'They hated rehearsals in Miami and just walked in out of the pool.'

'A famous picture of a famous picture being taken. This shot was eventually used on the cove of Life magazine. They couldn believe that photographer was using flash in the middle of th day.'

'Berry Gordy of Tamla Motown came down and the boys insisted on being photographed with him. Yet another souvenir.'

102

'Some girls came autograph hunting in the sea and of course The Beatles wanted something else from them. It made them laugh though!'

'I knew that lose or win (with Sonnie Liston) Cassius Clay would be a star, so we went to his gym in Miami. He was marvellous considering he had no idea who The Beatles were. But his manager had heard of them and when he found out they came from England, he did whatever they wanted. I only wish I'd had a movie camera, to film their simulated fights.'

'The hairdressing salon of the Hotel Deauville, where Sonnie Liston's wife worked.'

'Everywhere people were Beatle-crazy. Even at the gas stations in Miami they were wearing Beatle wigs.'

'The second Ed Sullivan appearance, live from Miami. They just never got tired, for them this wasn't work, it was enjoyment.'

RETURNING FROM US KENNEDY
AIRPORT TO LONDON HEATHROW,
22 FEBRUARY, 1964:

*'The Heathrow airport
authorities decided to investigate
how so many people got on to
the tarmac. They used these
pictures as testimony and I
believe there were a few sackings
as a result.'*

Twickenham, March 1964: Filming "A Hard Day's Night": *'The whole Ready Steady Go stage was reconstructed for the film sequence and The Beatles were made to dress in clothes they never normally wore.'*

'She was an extra, but the picture captures perfectly the twinkle in John's eye, that was so typical of him. It was here that John and I had an argument which meant I saw less and less of them. He began not to trust anybody, believing they were being fleeced by everybody. And because he was taking drugs, his paranoia was worsened. That day, he actually accused me of making a fortune out of The Beatles, while they saw nothing.'

'Paul half-heartedly hides from
the camera with Jane Asher.'

'Julie Andrews and Dick Van Dyke were filming "Mary Poppins" at the same studios.'

'A trailer for "A Hard Day's Night", serious faces on a ridiculous set.'

109

ABBEY ROAD, FEBRUARY, MARCH, APRIL, 1964: RECORDING "A HARD DAY'S NIGHT":
'And so Ringo started the ring fashion...'

"Around The Beatles". ATV
Wembley, 6 May, 1964:

Outside the National Portrait
Gallery, London. May, 1964:
*'I happened to spot these as I
walked past. Later, I would look
at John's face next to Kennedy's
and feel it was more than
coincidental.'*

113

LONDON PALLADIUM, 'NIGHT OF 100
STARS', 23 JULY, 1964:
*'They were impressed by
Laurence Olivier, but John was
keen to speak to me as this was
the first time we'd met since the
argument.'*

OPERA HOUSE, BLACKPOOL,
26 JULY, 1964:
'Yet another 'Beatle-iner.'

'One of Paul's favourite poses, I have so many pictures like this.'

THE BEATLES CHRISTMAS SHOW,
HAMMERSMITH ODEON, LONDON
24 DECEMBER, 1964 -
16 JANUARY 1965:
*'The back row consists of
Fourmost members, Dakotas
and Barron Knights. Centre
row: Fourmost member, Tommy
Quickly, Billy J. Kramer, Rolf
Harris, Cilla Black, Fourmost
member. The Beatles in front.'*

*'After the photocall comedian
Rolf Harris demonstrated his
strength on a cardboard Ringo.
They enjoyed Christmas Shows
because they were family
occasions, and during the couple
of years they had existed there
had been scarcely one boy at
their live shows. So the
Christmas Shows were a
pleasant change.'*

ABBEY ROAD, FEBRUARY-MARCH, 1965. RECORDING "HELP":
'John's Triumph Herald car.

'John is smiling right at me but you could never tell — like a dog who has rabies, you never knew when he would jump and bite.'

118

FILMING "HELP" AT TWICKENHAM
STUDIOS, FEBRUARY-APRIL, 1965:
*'Director Dick Lester stays
solemn in the background.'*

*'No press, no photos. They were
under terrible strain while they
were filming.'*

*'Paul with his younger brother
Mike McGear in the yard at
Twickenham studios solving a
family problem.'*

'John allowed Chris Denning of
Radio Luxembourg to interview
him briefly.'

THE ROYAL VARIETY CLUB LUNCH,
JUNE, 1965:
*'Paul was the only Beatle there
and was pleased they'd seated
him next to David Frost.'*

THE MBE PRESS CONFERENCE AT
THE SAVILLE THEATRE,
26 OCTOBER, 1965:
*'Witty repartee soon turned sour
when other recipients returned
their honours as protest against
The Beatles, and John
eventually returned his too,
although he regretted it.'*

123

BBC Playhouse Theatre,
Charing Cross, London:
'With Brian Matthew before the
performance. They became
easier and easier to work with.
They knew me so well I just had
to raise a finger or an eyebrow
and they'd know what I wanted,
I never had to shout.'

JULY 2, 1964:
THE BEATLES ARRIVE BACK IN
BRITAIN AFTER THEIR TOUR OF
THE FAR EAST, AUSTRALIA AND
NEW ZEALAND.
(OPPOSITE PAGE) LEAVING THE
PLANE WHILE DEREK TAYLOR
(RIGHT) THEIR PRESS OFFICER
LOOKS ON.

AUSTRALIAN APPLES PROMOTION
ADVERTISEMENT, APRIL, 1965: